Children Aflame with The Spirit

Amazing Historical Accounts
of
Wesleyan-Methodist Revivals
and
Modern Revivals with Children
in the Ministry
of
David Walters

Children Aflame with the Spirit of God

International Standard Book Number: 0-9629559-6-5

Published by Good News Fellowship Ministries
220 Sleepy Creek Road
Macon, GA 31210

DEDICATION

This booklet is dedicated to the memory of John Wesley and to all children everywhere. I pray that you, the reader, will not receive a lesser impartation and revelation of what God really has for us all in these days. Children, you are precious to God and His awesome power is available to you also.

Like my own daughters, I desire that you fulfill your destiny and be used by the Lord in a very wonderful and powerful way.

My special thanks to Author and Historian, Harry Sprange who made this book possible by supplying me with these litle known journels of John Wesley.

Harry Sprange resides in Scotland and is the author of 'Children in Revival' '300 hundred years of God's work in Scotland.' This book can be found on Amazon.

INTRODUCTION

For many years I have been preaching that children can know and experience God in a wonderful way and from a very young age. I have told pastors, teachers and parents that it is time to take God seriously in His dealings with our children. I have attempted to encourage and exhort Christians to begin to line up with God's vision for our youngsters, and not take the traditional Church view. This time I am shouting it! My desire and passion is that this booklet gets into the hand of every church leader, Sunday school teacher, youth and children's pastor, Christian educator and parent in this country.

Today, many men are making a commitment to God to be the husband and father that He requires them to be as they take part in "Promise Keepers" and other organizations. I pray that they will see what their part is in raising their children up to fulfill their destiny in God. Parents!

> "Train up a *child* in the way that he should go and when he is old he will not depart from it."
> **Proverbs 22:6**

Then Peter said to them:

> "Repent, and let every one of you be baptized in the name of Jesus Christ for the remission of sins, and you shall receive the gift of the Holy Spirit. For the promise is to you and *to your children...*"   **Acts 2:37&38**

4

In this exciting account of John Wesley's journals I have kept as close as possible to the original writings, changing only a few words, making it easier to understand for the modern reader. Some of the grammar and spelling is different from our present day English. *I have also taken the liberty of emphasizing the ages of the children and also some of the effects that the Holy Spirit had upon them.*

A number of years ago, my family and I were ministering in England. We visited a little house in Devon where John Wesley used to lodge. The little cottage had one room upstairs and one room downstairs. He slept in one room and met in the other room with about a dozen or so of the Methodist circuit preachers. While we were there we sensed the anointing of Wesley. We prayed for the same anointing and passion that he had in his day.

The following year I was again in England by myself. I visited a couple for lunch in the Bristol area whose family had a farm that dated back more than three hundred years. They showed me their grandmother's four-poster bed, which they said John Wesley once slept in. I took pleasure in videoing the house and the bed, thinking again of that great Methodist preacher. The material from his journals that is in this booklet had not been given to me at that time. Only recently did I obtain the extracts relating to children from his journals.

I had little idea that the same manisfestations that we have seen through the years in our own meetings with children also happened in his day. His writings have inspired me to believe for greater and deeper moves of God upon children and teens in our own ministry. I am not satisfied yet with what we have seen, and I believe that I have held back somewhat in being too radical and strong for fear of offending or causing problems to other Christians. I now feel that God is stirring me up to pull all the stops out and believe for mighty outpourings upon children, youth and families. If some religious folk oppose me, so be it. God will have His way.

* * * * * * * * * * * * * * * *

John Wesley's Journals References to Children

In the 1700's, many children died through plagues and diseases. Doctors weren't knowledgeable in treating people. Also, clean bodies, clean water and food were not regarded as important regarding health. Although Wesley prayed for the sick, there was not a great revelation regarding divine healing in that period of history.

29/5/1737. Indeed about this time we observed the Spirit of God move upon the minds of **many of the children.** They began more carefully to attend to the things that were spoken, both at home and at church, and a remarkable seriousness appeared in their whole behavior and conversation.

20/5/17930. In the evening I was interrupted at Nicholas Street, almost as soon as I began to speak, by the cries of one who as "pricked at the heart", and strongly groaned for pardon and peace. Another person dropped down and then a **little boy** near him was seized in the same manner.

17/7/1743. "On Saturday, S—-T—-, then about **ten years old,** walked in perfect health. She had never had any fits of any kind, nor any considerable sickness. About six in the morning she was rising, and inwardly praying to God, when suddenly she was seized with a violent trembling. Quickly after she lost her speech: in a few minutes her hearing: then her sight, and at the same time all sense and motion. Her mother immediately sent to the school for Mrs. Designe. At the same time her father, sent for Mr. Smith, apothecary, who lived near. At first, he proposed bleeding her immediately, and applying a large blister. But upon examining her further he said, "It signifies nothing, the child is dead." About twelve o'clock she began to stir; then she opened her eyes, and gave the following account:—

As soon as I lost my senses, I was in a dismal place, full of briers, and pits, and ditches, stumbling up and down, and not knowing where to turn, or which way to go either forward or backward; and it was almost quite dark, there being but a little faint twilight, so that I could scarce see before me. I was crying ready to break my heart; and a man came to me and said, 'Child, where are you going?'

I said, 'I could not tell.'

He said, 'What do you want?'

I answered, 'I want Christ to be my refuge.'

He said, 'What is your name?' And I told him.

But I did not tell him S—-T—-. I told him a name which I never heard before.

He said, 'You are the child for whom I am sent. You are to go with me.'

I saw it grew lighter as he spoke. We walked together till we came to a stile. He went over, and bid me stay a little. I staid about half a quarter of an hour.

8

And then I observed his clothes. They reached down to his feet, and were shining and white as snow.

Then he came back, and kneeled down and prayed. You never heard such a prayer in your life. Afterward he said, 'Come with me.'

I went over the stile, and it was quite light. He brought me through a narrow lane, into a vast broad road, and told me, 'This leads to hell; but be not afraid, you are not to stay there.'

At the end of that road a man stood clothed like the other, in white shining clothes, which reached down to the ground. None could pass in or out, without his knowledge. But he had not the key. The man that was with me carried the key, and unlocked the door, and we went in together.

For a little way we walked straight forward: then turning to the left hand, we went down a very high, steep hill. I could scarce bear the stench and smoke of brimstone.

I saw a vast many people that seemed to be chained down, crying and gnashing their teeth. The man told me, the sins they delighted in once, they are tormented with now. I saw a vast number who stood up cursing and blaspheming God, and spitting at each other. And many were making balls of fire, and throwing them at one another. I saw many others who had cups of fire, out of which they were drinking down flames. And others who held cards of fire in their hands, and seemed to be playing with them.

We staid there I thought for about half an hour. Then my guide said, 'Come, I will show you now a glorious place.'

I walked with him till we came into a narrow road, in which we could hardly walk abreast. This brought us into a great broad place. And I saw the gate of heaven, which stood wide open; but it was so bright, I could not look at it long.

We went straight in, and walked through a large place, where I saw saints and angels: and through another large place, where were an abundance more. They were all of one height and stature. And when one prayed they all prayed, when one sang they all sang. And they all sang alike, with a smooth, even voice, not one higher or lower than another.

We went through this into a third place. There I saw God sitting upon His throne. It was a throne of light, brighter than the sun. I could not fix my eyes upon it. I saw three, but all as one. Our Saviour held a pen in His hand.

A great book lay at His right side, another at His left, and a third partly behind Him. In the first He set down the prayers and good works of His people. In the second He set down all the curses, and all the evil works of the wicked. I saw the He discerns the whole earth at a glance. And He discerns the whole heavens. At once He beholds earth and heaven with one look.

Then our Lord took the first book in His hand, and went and said, 'Father, Behold the prayers and works of my people.'

And He held up His hands, and prayed, and interceded to His Father for us. I never heard any voice like that. But I cannot tell how to explain it. And His Father said, 'Son I forgive Thy people; not for their sake, but Thine.'

Then our Lord wrote it down in the third book, and returned to His throne rejoicing with the host of heaven.

It seemed to me as if I stayed here several months. But I never slept all the while; and there was no night; and I saw no sky or sun, but clear light everywhere.

Then we went back to a large door, which my guide opened, and we walked into pleasant gardens, by brooks and fountains.

As we walked, I said, 'I did not see my brother here;' (who died sometime before)

He said, 'Child, thou canst not know thy brother yet; because thy breath remains in thy body. Thy spirit is to return to the earth. Thou must watch and pray; and when thy breath leaves thy body, thou shall come again hither, and be joined to these, and know everyone as before.'

I said, 'When is that to be?'

He said, 'I know not; nor any angel in heaven, but God alone.'

Then he took me into another pleasant garden, where were all manner of fruits.

He told me, 'This garden bears fruit always.'

Here I saw a glorious place, which had large gold letters written over the door. He bid me read; and I read, 'This is a fountain for sin and uncleanness for My people. At what time soever they will return, they shall be cleansed from all their idols.'

The door stood open, and I looked in, and I saw, as it were, a great cistern full of water, white as milk. We seemed to walk up and down in this garden for some weeks, and he told me what everything meant. I never wanted to eat or drink, nor felt any weariness.

While we were walking he said, 'Sing.'

I said, "What shall I sing?"

And he said, 'Sing praises unto the King of the place.'

I sung several verses. Then he said, 'I must go.' I would have fain gone with him; but he said, 'Your time is not yet: you have more work to do upon the earth.'

Immediately he was gone; and I came to myself and began to speak."

Her mother told me further, 'As soon as ever Kitty recovered her speech, she gave me just the same account; adding, 'I have heard the finest hymn you ever heard in your life.' She then sung three verses, the most solid, awful* words which I have ever heard. Kitty continued speaking many awful words, with many sighs and tears: till about three in the afternoon, she fell into a slumber, which continued till seven. Then she spoke the same things to Mrs. Designe; after which she was silent, till about five in the morning."

(*Awful—full of awe, wonder)

* * * * * * * * * * * * * * * *

Some time ago I was ministering in a church were the Spirit was moving upon **many children.** A little boy of about **seven years old** was lying down under the power of the Spirit. I was ministering to other children and after about twenty minutes he began to cry out. His voice became stronger and louder, and he began to scream, "My legs! My legs! They are burning! They are burning!"

Immediately, concerned adults came around him and began to pray. I came over the picked him up in my arms and told the tormenting spirit to leave and for the peace of God to come upon him. Suddenly his whole countenance changed to a beautiful smile of peace. I put him back down on the floor and carried on ministering to the other children. After about half an hour he came to himself and asked me if he could tell what had happened to him. I replied, Go ahead."

He said, "I found myself in hell, and there were terrible flames that were burning my legs. There were also horrible creatures with great claws that began to tear at my legs; the pain was awful. As you prayed for me I suddenly left that horrible place and found myself in heaven. It was beautiful and I felt a great peace. I saw many things, including my uncle and my grandfather."
                                                    --- DAVID WALTERS

16/9/1744. I buried, near the same place, one who has soon finished her course, going to God in the full assurance of faith, when she was little more than *four years old.*

In her last sickness she spent intervals of her convulsions in speaking to God; and when she perceived her strength to be near exhausted, she desired all the family to come near, and prayed for them all, one by one; then for her Ministers, for the Church, and for all the world. A short time after, recovering from a fit, she lifted up her eyes, said, 'Thy kingdom come,' and died.

28/4/1746. I inquired more particularly of Mrs. Nowens, concerning her *little son.* She said, 'He appeared to have a continual fear of God, and an awful sense of His presence; that he frequently went to prayers by himself, and prayed for his father, and many others by name; that he had an exceeding great tenderness of conscience, being sensible of the least sin, and crying and refusing to be comforted, when he thought that he had in anything displeased God; that a few days since he broke out into prayer aloud, and then said,

'Mama, I shall go to heaven soon, and be with the little angels; and you will be there too, and my papa; but you will not go so soon;'

The day before, he went to a *little girl* and said, 'Polly, you and I must go to prayers: Don't mind your doll: Kneel down now I must go to prayers, God bids me."

When the Holy Ghost teaches, is there any delay in learning?" This **child** was then just *three years old.* A year or two later he died in peace.

* * * * * * * * * * * * * * * *

We have just seen from the last account a small boy encouraging a **little girl** to put away her doll and go to pray. I was recently ministering in a church in Scotland. While I was preaching I saw a girl about seven years old, playing with a "Game Boy" portable video. Her mother was aware of what the girl was doing, but did not seem bothered. I addressed them both and said that it was not the time to play or allow our children to play with games. A few days later the elders of the church wrote me a letter of rebuke, saying I had not right to correct their church members in such a way, especially as they had given permission for children to play with games and toys in the church meetings. It seems that the little boy in Wesley's account was more spiritual than the elders of that church.

—DAVID WALTERS

29/5/1750. (KINSALE, NEAR CORK) I enquired concerning Richard Hutchinson, of whom I had heard many speak. His mother informed me, "It was August last, being then above *four years old,* that he began to talk much of God, and to ask abundance of questions concerning Him. From that time he never played or laughed, but was as serious as one of threescore. He constantly reproved any that cursed or swore, or spoke indecently in his hearing, and frequently mourned over his brother, who was two or three years older, saying 'I fear my brother will go to hell, for he does not love God.'

Four days after he fell ill with small-pox; and was light headed almost as soon as he was taken, but all his incoherent sentences were either exhortation, or pieces of hymns, or prayer. The worse he was, the most earnest he was to die, saying 'I must go home.'

One said, 'You are at home.'

He earnestly replied, 'No this is not my home; I will go to heaven.'

On the tenth day of his illness he raised himself up and said, 'Let me go; let me go to my Father: I will go home: now, now I will go to my Father.' After which he lay down and died.'

8/4/1755. (DEATH AT HAYFIELD OF A LITTLE GIRL) She spoke exceedingly plain, yet very seldom; and then only a few words. She was scarce ever seen to she could not bear any that did, or behaved in a light or unserious manner. If her brother or sister spoke angrily to each other, or behaved triflingly, she either sharply reproved, (when that seemed needful) or tenderly entreated them to give over. If she spoke too sharply to any, she would humble herself to them, and not rest until they had forgiven her. After her health declined she was particularly pleased with hearing that hymn sung "Abba, Father" and would be frequently singing that line herself, "Abba, Father, hear me cry."

On Monday April the 7th, without any struggle, she fell asleep, having lived **two years and six months.**

11/4/1756. (DUBLIN) I met about a **hundred children,** who are catechized (instructed) publicly twice a week. Thomas Walsh began this some months ago, and the fruit of it appears already. What a pity, that all our preachers, in every place, have not the zeal and wisdom to follow his example.

30/7/1758. (CORK) I began meeting with the **children** in the afternoon, though with little hopes of doing them good; but I had not spoken long on our natural state before many of them were in tears, and five or six so affected, that they could not refrain from crying aloud to God. When I began praying, their cries increased, so that my voice was soon lost. I have seen no such work among *children* for eighteen or nineteen years.

* * * * * * * * * * * * * * * * *

It is worth noting that Wesley preached to children and was often surprised at the effect. There are many pastors today who would never dream of preaching to the children in their church. They don't even believe that children can respond to preaching; just give them stories, lessons and entertainment.

—DAVID WALTERS

* * * * * * * * * * * * * * * * *

4/5/1759. (THURSDAY) Mr. Berridge and I went to hear Mr. Hicks, at Wrestlingworth, four miles from Everton. We discoursed with him first, and were glad to hear he had wholly given himself up to the glorious work of God, and that the power of the Highest fell upon his hearers, as upon Mr. Berridge's.

While he was preaching, fifteen or sixteen persons felt the arrows of the Lord, and dropped down. A few of these cried out with the utmost violence, and little intermission, for some hours; while the rest made no great noise, but continued struggling, as in the pangs of death.

I observed, besides these, *one **little girl*** deeply convinced, and a ***boy, nine or ten years old.*** Both these, and several others, when carried into the parsonage-house, either lay as dead, or struggled with all their might; but in a short time, their cries increased beyond measure, so that the loudest singing could scarce be heard.

Some at last called on me to pray, which I did, and for a time all were calm; but the storm soon began again. Mr. Hicks then prayed and afterward Mr. Berridge; but still, remained in deep sorrow of heart.

* * * * * * * * * * * * * * * *

There have been many occasions when we have observed children of all ages, from **three years to teenagers,** come under the power of the Holy Spirit.

Some of them have been on the floor for hours in various degrees of experiences from speaking in tongues, crying, laughing, trembling, and shaking. The Holy Spirit keeping a child's hands raised up toward heaven for one or two hours. Often their faces have lit up with a heavenly glow. Some of the very small children have drawn pictures of heaven and angels to show their teachers what they saw during those experiences. Parents at later times testified of the changes wrought in their children's behavior after being touched by God.

—DAVID WALTERS

* * * * * * * * * * * * * * * *

TUESDAY 17TH. After preaching, Mr. B was lively and strong, so that the closeness of a crowded room neither affected his breath nor hindered his rejoicing over **two children, one about eight, the other about six years old,** who were crying aloud to God for mercy. I observed also a *beggar girl, seven or eight years old,* who had scarce any clothes, but a ragged piece of old rug. She too had felt the Word of God as a two-edged sword, and mourned to be covered with Christ's righteousness...

SUNDAY 22ND. (GRANDCHESTER) the *little child* before mentioned continues to astonish all the neighborhood. A noted physician came some time ago, and closely examined her. The result was, he confessed, 'It was no distemper of mind, but the hand of God.' About this time the work of God exceedingly increased under the Rev. Berridge, near Everton. I cannot give a clearer view of this than by transcribing part of an eye witness:

SUNDAY, MAY 20TH. Being with Mr. Berridge at Everton, I was much fatigued and did not rise. But Mr. Berridge did, and observed several faintings and crying out while he was preaching. Afterwards at church, I heard many cry out, *especially* **children** whose agonies were amazing: one of the eldest, ***a girl ten or twelve years old,*** was full in my view, in violent contortions of body and weeping aloud, I think incessantly during the whole service.

Several much **younger children** were in Mr. Berridge's view agonizing as this did. The church was equally crowded in the afternoon, the windows being filled within and without, and even the outside of the pulpit to the very top; so that Mr. Berridge seemed almost stifled by their breath. Yet, feeble and sickly as he is he was continually strengthened, and his voice for the most part was distinguishable, in the midst of all the outcries....

The greatest number of them who cried or fell were men: but some women, and **several children,** felt the power of the same almighty Spirit as seemed just sinking into hell. This occasioned a mixture of various sounds; some shrieking, some roaring aloud. The most general was a loud breathing, like people half strangled and gasping for life; and indeed almost all the cries were like those of human creatures dying in bitter anguish.

Great numbers wept without any noise; others fell down as dead; some sinking in silence; some with extreme noise and agitation. I stood on the pew seat, as did a young man in the opposite pew, an able-bodied, fresh, healthy countryman, but in a moment, while he seemed to think nothing less, down he dropped with a violence inconceivable. The adjoining pews seemed shook with his fall. I heard afterwards the stamping of feet, ready to break the boards, as he lay in strong convulsions.

Among several that were struck down in the next pew, was a girl who was violently seized as him. When he fell, Mr. Berridge and I felt our souls thrilled with a momentary dread, as when one is killed by a cannonball, another often feels the wind of it.

Among *the* **children** who felt the arrows of the Almighty, I saw a sturdy **boy,** about **eight years old, who roared** above his fellows, and seemed in his agony to struggle with the strength of a grown man. His face was red as scarlet; and almost all on whom God laid His hand, turned either very red or almost black.

When I returned, after a little walk to Mr. Berridge's house, I found it full of people. He was fatigued, but said, he would nevertheless give them a word of exhortation. I stayed in the next room and saw the **girl** that I had observed so particularly distressed in the church, lying on the floor as one dead, but without any ghastliness in her face. ...

After a while she began to stir. She was then set in a chair; and after sighing awhile, suddenly rose up, rejoicing in God. Her face was covered with the most beautiful smile I ever saw. She frequently fell on her knees, but was generally running to and fro, speaking these and the like words: 'O what can Jesus do for lost sinners! He has forgiven all my sins! I am in heaven! I am in heaven! O how He loves me! And how I love Him!'

6/8/1759. EVERTON. I talked with Ann Thorn and two others who had been several times in trances. They were exceptions; but, in general, from that moment, they were in another world, knowing nothing of what was done or said by all that were round about them.

Alice Miller, **_fifteen years old_** had fallen into a trance. I went down immediately, and found her sitting on a stool, and leaning against the wall, with her eyes open and fixed upward. I made a motion as if going to strike; but she continued immovable.

Her face showed an unspeakable mixture of reverence and love, while silent tears stole down her cheeks. Her lips were a little open, and sometimes moved; but not enough to cause any sound. I do not know whether I ever saw a human face look so beautiful. Sometimes it was covered with a smile, as from joy mixing with love and reverence, but the tears fell still, though not so fast.

In about half an hour I observed her countenance change into the form of fear, pity, and distress. Then she burst into a flood of tears, and cried out,

"Dear Lord, they will be damned! They will be all damned!"

But in about five minutes her smile returned and only love and joy appeared on her face. This was repeated several times; about seven, her senses returned.

I asked, 'Where have you been?'

'I have been with my Saviour. In heaven or on earth; I cannot tell; but I was in glory!'

'Why then did you cry?'

'Not for myself; but for the world; for I saw they were on the brink of hell.'...

ABOUT THREE WEEKS BEFORE CHRISTMAS 1768. William Cooper at Walsal, in Staffordshire then **nine years old** was convinced of sin and would frequently say, he should go to hell and the devil would fetch him. But in about two weeks it pleased God to reveal His pardoning love. Billy's mouth was then filled with praise, declaring to all what God had done for him.

Billy was awakened, God was pleased to convince his sister Lucy, then **eleven years old.** He soon put a song of praise into her mouth also, so that they might rejoice together in God their Saviour. At the same time they were both heavily afflicted in their bodies. But so much more was the power of God manifested, causing them to continue in the triumph of faith throughout their sharpest pains.

On December 30th one of their sisters was coming to see them. Billy told her, that he has been very ill; but, said he,

'I do not mean in my body, but in my soul; I felt my sins so heavy, that I thought I should go to hell, and I saw the devil ready to drag me away. Nay, for a week, I thought myself just in the flames of hell. The sins that troubled me most were, telling lies and quarreling with my sister. I saw, if God did not forgive me I was lost. And I knew, quarreling was as great a sin in Lucy as in me; and if she did not get a pardon, and feel the love of Jesus, she could not go to heaven.'

Lucy said, 'When I heard Mr. A describe two sorts of people, one sort washed in the blood of Christ, and the other not, I found I was not, and therefore if I died so, I must go to hell.'

Being asked what sin lay most on her conscience, she replied, 'Taking His Name in vain by repeating prayers, when I did not think of God.'

When Billy was confessing that he loved money,

Lucy said, 'And so did I; and was angry if I had not as much as Billy. I loved money more than God, and He might justly have sent me to hell for it.'

When Billy was asked how he knew his sins were forgiven?

He answered, 'Christ told me so. I had a great struggle in my heart with the devil and sin, till it pleased Jesus to come into my soul. I now feel His love in my heart, and He tells me He has forgiven my sins.'

Being asked how He did?

He replied, 'Happy in Jesus: Jesus is sweet to my soul.'

'Do you choose to live or die?'

He answered, 'Neither: I hope, if I live, I shall praise God: and if I die, I am sure I shall go to Him; for He has forgiven my sins, and given me His love.'

One asked Lucy how long she had been in the triumph of faith? She answered, 'Only this week; before I had much to do with satan: but now Jesus has conquered him for me.'

While she was speaking; feeling great pain of body, she said, 'Oh I want more of these pains, more of these pains, to bring me nearer to Jesus.' Speaking of knowing the voice of Christ, she said, 'The voice of Christ is a strange voice to them who do not know their sins forgiven: but I know it; for He has pardoned all my sins, and given me His love. And Oh what a mercy, that such a hell-deserving wretch as me, should be made to taste of His love.'

Billy had frequent fits. When he found one coming, he with a smile laid down his head, saying, 'Oh sweet love!' or, 'Oh sweet Jesus!'

And as soon as he came to himself, being asked how he did? he would reply, "I am happy in the love of Christ."

One night a gentleman and his wife came to see them, and the gentlewoman looking on Lucy said, "She looks as if nothing was the matter with her; she is so pleasant to the eyes."

Lucy replied, "I have enough to make me look so; for I am full of the love of God."

25

While she spoke, her eyes sparkled exceedingly, and the tears flowed down from her cheeks. At this, Billy smiled, but could not speak; having been speechless for more than an hour.

It seemed he was just going into eternity; but the Lord revived him a little, and as soon as he could speak, he desired to be held up in bed, and looked at the gentlemen, who asked how he did?

He answered, "I am happy in Christ, and I hope you are."

He said, "I hope I can say I am."

Billy replied, "Has Christ pardoned your sins?" He said, "I hope He has."

"Sir," said Billy, "Hope will not do. For I had this hope, and yet if I had died then, I should surely have gone to hell. But He has forgiven me all my sins, and given me the taste of His love. If you have this love, you will know it and be sure of it; but you cannot know it without the power of God.

You may read as many books about Christ as you please, (the man was a great reader) but if you read all your life, this will only be in your head, and that head will perish. So that if you have not the love of God in your heart you will go to hell. But I hope you will not; I will pray to God for you, that He may give you His love."

A young woman speaking to them for the second time was addressed by Billy.

"Miss are you assured of your interest in Christ?"

She answered, "I hope I am in Christ; but assurance is no way essential."

He replied, "But if you have His love, you will be sure you have it. You will know it in your heart. I am afraid your hope is only in your head. Do you never quarrel with anybody?"

She said, "No."

"But," says he, "You quarrel with God's word; out of His hand; and you say the world will; so you make God a story-teller;" at this she went away displeased.

When they were asked, if they were afraid to die?

They always answered, "No; for what can death do? He can only lay his cold hand upon our bodies."

One told Lucy, "Now you may live as you please since you are sure of going to heaven."

She replied, "No I would not sin against my dear Saviour, even if you would give me this room full of gold."

On the Monday before Billy died, he repeated that hymn, with the most triumphant joy:—

> *"Come let us join our cheerful songs*
> *With the angels round the throne!"*

27

Afterwards he repeated the Lord's prayer. The last words he spoke intelligibly were, "How pleasant is it to be with Christ for ever and ever, for ever and ever! Amen! Amen! Amen!"

While he lay speechless, there came into the room some who he feared knew not God. He seemed much affected, wept and moaned much, waved his hand, and put it on his sister's mouth; intimating, as she supposed, that she should speak to them. On Wednesday evening, February 1st, his happy spirit returned to God. Lucy died not long after.

* * * * * * * * * * * * * * * *

A **ten year old boy** came to a conference I was speaking at. During that time the Lord impressed him to witness to all the children in his neighborhood, school and town. Then God would send him to be a missionary to the nations. Over the next two years his parents confirmed that he had led over a **hundred children** to the Lord.
—DAVID WALTERS

* * * * * * * * * * * * * * * *

5/10/1765. I spent some time with the children at Kingswood. They are all in health; they behave well; they learn well. But, alas! except for two or three, there is no life in them.

* * * * * * * * * * * * * * * *

Here again is a warning for Christian parents and those involved in Christian education. We cannot be merely content with raising good children; we must seek to raise godly, anointed ones that **know** their God. It is so easy to be content with your children "Having a form of godliness, but denying its power." (See 2 Timothy 3:5.)

—DAVID WALTERS

* * * * * * * * * * * * * * * * *

16/9/1770. KINGSWOOD SCHOOL. ...29TH SAT.
I was awaked between four and five, by the *children vehemently crying to God.* The maids went to them at five. And first one of the boys, then another, then one and another of the maids, earnestly poured out their souls before God, both for themselves and for the rest.

They continued weeping and praying till nine o'clock, not thinking about meat or drink, nay, Richard Piercy took no food all the day, but remained in words or groans calling upon God.

About one o'clock all the maids and three of the boys went upstairs and began praying again; and now they found the Lord's hand was not shortened; between two and three, many rejoiced with joy unspeakable. They all continued together till after four, praising the God of their salvation; indeed they seemed to have forgotten all things here below, and to think of nothing but God and heaven...

* * * * * * * * * * * * * * * * *

Some time ago I was in Vancouver, Canada. I was invited to speak at a **Christian School.** There were about one hundred and thirty students from **ages six through eighteen** that gathered together for the assembly. After some mild praise and worship I was invited to address them. I preached on "If anyone desires to come after me…." (Matt.16:24) and encouraged them to be totally sold out for Christ. There were also about forty Asian students at the assembly who were not saved.

At the end of the message I made an appeal for anyone who desired to receive Christ as their Saviour, but with no response. The Asians did not budge. I then exhorted the professing Christians to rededicate their lives to the Lord and a large crowd came forward from every age group. I prayed for the students and asked God to touch them in a special way. I then sat down with the principal and waited for the Holy Spirit to move.

After about ten minutes the Lord moved on a **fifteen- year- old girl.** She began to pray against the demonic strongholds over the children, their school, and their homes.

She then went up to a teenage boy of about sixteen, and laid hands on him and began to pray. Suddenly he fell to the floor and received a mighty deliverance. He then rose up, filled with the Holy Spirit and began to go and pray and minister to the Asian students. Within a short time they received deliverance, salvation, and the fullness of the Holy Spirit.

The flame began to spread and within a short time all the children from 1st grade through 12th grade were in circles praying for each other. Many were crying out to God. Teachers came in to watch and began to weep as they saw God move upon the children. This went on for about two hours and almost every student was affected. Suddenly, some of the students began singing praises to God with great passion, raising their hands and falling on their knees. After a time, one of them stood up and said,

"Let us march around the school and take it for Jesus!"

The principal told me that the **fifteen-year-old** girl whom God had used was slightly retarded and was regarded by the other students as being socially unacceptable.

"But God has chosen the foolish things of the world to put to shame the wise..." (**1 Cor. 1:27**)

* * * * * * * * * * * * * * * *

27/1/1771. I buried the remains of Joan Turner, who spent all her last hours in rejoicing and praising God, and died full of faith and of the Holy Ghost, at **three and half years old.**

17/1/1772. (HERTFORD) I found the **poor children** whom Mr. A kept at school were increased to about thirty boys and thirty girls. I went in immediately to the girls. As soon as I began to speak, some of them burst into tears, and their emotions rose higher and higher. But it was kept within bounds until I began to pray.

A cry then arose, which spread from one to another, till almost all cried aloud for mercy, and would not be comforted. But how the scene was changed when I went to the boys! They seemed as dead as stones, and scarce appeared to mind anything that was said, nay, some of them could hardly refrain from laughter.

However, I spoke on, and set before them the terrors of the Lord. Presently one was cut to the heart, soon after another, and another. In ten minutes the far greater part of them were affected as the girls had been. Except at Kingswood, I have seen no such work of God upon children for above thirty years.

* * * * * * * * * * * * * * * *

At a conference in Illinois I was speaking to children when two little boys brought another little boy to me. He was about **five years of age.** "Mr. Walters! He can't talk!" they said.

The child looked very alarmed and was making grunting noises and pointing to his mouth.

"What do you mean he can't talk?" I said, "Has he always been like that?"

"No! He was talking all the time when you first began to preach."I addressed the little boy, "Were you saying silly things?" He nodded in agreement.

"Were you saying things that would displease God?" Again he nodded.

"Then you had better repent right away and tell God you are sorry."

He bowed his head and closed his eyes. I then prayed for him to have his voice restored. Suddenly, he lifted his head and with a big smile on his face and shouted out, "I can talk! I can talk!"

This demonstration of God's presence and power brought a spirit of reverence upon the children.

Laughing, mocking, and fooling around grieve the Holy Spirit of God. As in the days of Wesley, so it's happening today. God is not allowing the spirit of mockery or fooling around to prevail.

—DAVID WALTERS

* * * * * * * * * * * * * * * *

6/4/1772. (MANCHESTER) In the afternoon I drank tea at A.O. But how was I shocked. The *children that used to cling about me,* and drink in every word, had been to a boarding-school! There they had *unlearned all religion,* and even seriousness; and had learned pride, vanity, affectation, and whatever could guard them against the knowledge and love of God! Methodist parents, who would send your girls headlong to hell, send them to a fashionable boarding-school.

3/6/1772. WAREDALE...Margaret Spencer, *aged four-teen,* and Sally Blackburn, *a year younger* experienced salvation. But what a contrast was there between them! Sally Blackburn was all calmness; her look, her speech, her whole carriage, was as sedate as if she had lived three-score years.

On the contrary, Peggy was all fire; her eyes sparkled, her very features spoke, her whole face was alive; and she looked as if she was just ready to take wing for heaven! Lord, let neither of these live to dishonor Thee! Rather take them unspotted to Thyself!

5/6/1772.FROM AN ACCOUNT BY JOHN FENWICK. Of 165 members in their Society: "Forty three of these are *children, thirty of whom are rejoicing in the love of God.* The chief instrument God has used among these is Jane Salkeld, a school mistress; a young woman who is a pattern to all that believe.

A few of her children are:

Phebe Teatherston, *nine years old,* a child of uncommon understanding.

Hannah Watson, *ten years old,* full of faith and love;

Aaron Ridson, *not eleven years old,* but wise and staid as a man.

Sarah Smith, *eight and half years old,* but as serious as a woman of fifty.

Sarah Moris, *fourteen years of age,* is as a mother among them, always serious, always watching over the rest, and building them up in love."

[WESLEY THEN COMPARES IT TO EVERTON]

Yea, **many children** here have had far deeper experience, and more constant fellowship with God, than the oldest man or woman at Everton, which I have seen or heard of; so that, upon the whole, we may affirm, "Such a work of God as this has not been seen before in the three kingdoms."

12/6/1774. (WAREDALE) Afterwards I met the poor remains of the Select Society. But neither of my *two lovely children,* neither Peggy Spence nor Sally Blackburn were there. Indeed a whole row of such I had seen before; but three in four of them were now as careless as ever.

In the evening I sent for Peggy Spence and Sally Blackburn. Peggy came, and I found she had well-nigh regained her ground, walking in the light, and having a lively hope of recovering all that she had lost. Sally flatly refused to come, and then ran outside.

Being found at length, after a flood of tears, she was brought almost by force. But I could not get one look, and hardly a word from her. She seemed to have no hope left; yet she is not out of God's reach.

I now enquired into the cause of that grievous decay in the vast work of God which was here two years before. And I found several causes had concurred:

1. Not one of the preachers that succeeded was capable of being a *nursing father* to *newly-born children.*

2. Jane Salkeld, one great instrument in the work, marrying, was debarred from meeting the **young ones;** and there being none left, who so naturally cared for them, fell heaps upon heaps.

3. Most of the liveliest in the Society were the single men and women. And several of these in a little time contracted an inordinate affection for each other, whereby they so grieved the Holy Spirit of God that He in a great measure departed from them.

* * * * * * * * * * * * * * * *

Here is a warning for us to heed. The result of our own ministry to children has sometimes been hindered in churches because the move of God upon the hearts of the children ceased shortly after we had left. Leadership, children's teachers, and parents did not want to pay the price to develop the vision and encourage the children to pursue the ways of the Spirit. It was easier to go back to the old format of stories, games and videos. We have also known of churches that have removed anointed teachers from ministering to the children, because revival has broken out among the youngsters, and the leadership did not want them exposed to the supernatural power of God, often claiming it was disturbing the children's emotions.

—DAVID WALTERS

* * * * * * * * * * * * * * * *

4/9/1774. KINGSWOOD. On Saturday Ralph Mather met with the *children* and talked to three of them at about four in the afternoon. These freely confessed their besetting sins, and appeared greatly humbled. At five, *all the* **children** met in the school. During an examination then given, first one, then two or three, were much affected. Afterwards two more were *taken apart,* who were soon *deeply distressed;* and one of them, James (Whitestone), in less than half an hour, found a clear sense of the love of God. Near seven, there came down the **boys** in the school, and Mr. Mather asked, "Which of you will serve God?"

They all seemed *thunderstruck* and ten or twelve fell down upon their knees. Mr. Mather prayed, and then the boy, James Whitestone. Immediately one and another cried out, which brought in the other boys, who seemed struck more and more, till about thirty were kneeling and praying at once.

Before half an hour past nine, ten of them knew they were accepted in the Beloved. Several more were brought to birth.

5/19/1774. (SUNDAY) KINGSWOOD. I examined sixteen of them, who desired to partake of the Lord's Supper. Nine or ten who had a clear sense of the pardoning love of God. The others were fully determined never to rest till they could witness the same confession.

Eighteen of the children from that time met in three bands, besides twelve who met in a trial band. *These were remarkable for their love to each other, as well as for steady seriousness.*

They met every day; besides which, *all the* **children** met in class. Those **children** *who found peace* were:-

James Whitestone, Alexander Mather, Matthew Lowes, William Snowdon, John Keil, Charles Farr, John Hamilton, Benjamin Harris, and Edward Keil.

* * * * * * * * * * * * * * * *

In early 1970's in England I had my first opportunity to preach in a girl's public school. It was a small Christian Bible group of about fifteen teenage girls of whom some were not Christians. After I preached, about seven of them began to weep profusely, with great emotion. I was concerned because the classes were about to resume and the teacher was on her way back into the classroom.

The result of that encounter was that I was invited to preach to the whole school of some 1,200 girls and the Christian group grew from 15 to at least 150. This opened the doors of many schools and colleges in the town and also in other towns and cities across the country. During those years we witnessed many hundreds of children and teens come to salvation and the baptism of the Holy Spirit. There were also a number of teachers that found the Lord.

Surprisingly, a few years ago, speaking at a Christian school in Bristol, England, I was confronted by an irate teacher. She was very upset when some of the girls and boys that I had preached to had left the meeting weeping.

"What have you done with my children?" she asked.

"I just preached to them about Jesus," I answered.

Not understanding the operations of the Holy Spirit, she furiously replied, "Jesus is supposed to make people happy. You have made them into emotional wrecks!"

I wonder how she would have dealt with John Wesley!
—DAVID WALTERS

* * * * * * * * * * * * * * * *

12/5/1782. (SUNDAY) About eight I preached at Misterton; about one at Overthorpe. Many of the Epworth *children were there,* and their spirit spread to all around them; but the huge congregation was in the Market-place at Epworth, and the Lord, in the midst of them.

The love-feast which followed, exceeded all. I never knew such a one here before. As soon as one had done speaking, another began. *Several of them were children,* but they spoke with the wisdom of the aged, though with the fire of youth. So out of the mouth of babes and sucklings did God perfect praise.

8/6/1784. I CAME TO STOCKTON-ON-TEES. Here I found an uncommon work of God among the **children.** Many of them from **six to fourteen years,** were under serious impressions, and earnestly desirous to save their souls. There were upwards of sixty who constantly came to be examined and appeared to be greatly awakened. I preached at noon on, "The Kingdom of heaven is at hand"; and the people seemed to feel every word, one of whom and another sunk down upon their knees, until they were all kneeling; so I knelt down myself, and began praying for them. Abundance of people ran back into the house. The fire kindled and ran from heart to heart, till few, if any, were unaffected.

Is not this a new thing in the earth? **God begins His work in children.** Thus it has also been in Cornwall, Manchester, and Epworth. Thus the flame spreads to those of riper years; till at length they all know Him, and praise Him, from the least unto the greatest.

* * * * * * * * * * * * * * * * * * * *

Some years ago my wife Kathie and I were ministering to teens at a family camp outside Columbus, Ohio. Many of the teenagers were rebellious toward the things of God. We felt to minister one time to the younger children.

We gathered the **5–11 year olds** after supper and prayed for them for the anointing. There were approximately 30 children present. After I had prayed I sat down and waited for God to touch them. They stood around in silence. After about 10 minutes the Holy Spirit came strongly upon a little girl of about **six years old.** She fell to her knees and began to weep. Then one by one, other children also fell to their knees and began to weep.

After a while they stood up with hands raised and began to sing in the Spirit and worship the Lord, tears still coursing down their cheeks. A little while later they bowed down again shipping and then praying and interceding. Intermittently, they stood and then bowed down. Some began to speak in other tongues, prophesy and have visions. One small boy of **eight years** had a detailed prophetic vision of the U.S.

The chapel bell rang for the evening family service. The chapel was at the top of a hill and the children began to climb up, holding on to each other, as many were still under the influence of the Spirit. Halfway up the hill, the young children caught up with the reluctant teenagers, who were dragging their feet to the meeting. As the children came alongside the teens, the power of God fell upon them. They in turn fell to their knees and began to cry out to God. The smaller children laid hands on them and prayed and the teenagers were delivered from their rebellion and bondage and received the Baptism of the Holy Spirit.

The guest speaker was preparing his message and the musicians were practicing their songs. When all of the young peo- ple entered into the chapel, the Spirit of God fell powerfully upon the whole place. Many adults simply fell off their seats and received physical healings and the infilling of the Holy Spirit. That night the speaker was unable to preach his message and the musicians never sang their prepared songs. God just took over. As in John Wesley's meeting on Stockton-on-Tees, **God began His work in the children.**

On another occasion my wife and I were ministering at an Easter retreat held at a Christian guest house on the Isle of Wight, a small island off the south coast of England. The weekend was coming to a close, signifying the ending of the retreat.

On the Sunday evening we had met for praise and ministry in the chapel, attached to the guest-house. When the meeting finished the adults and children went into the house for refreshments. The teenagers were left in the chapel still standing in a circle and singing praise songs to the Lord.

After about 30 minutes a teenager came running in shouting, *"David! David! Come quickly!"*

I went back into the chapel. A strange sight met my eyes as I entered. In the middle of the room was a young lad of about sixteen who had received salvation earlier that day. He was surrounded by a circle of teenagers. He was kneeling with his right arm and index finger extended and appeared to be in a trance. He slowly pointed around the room to each one of the teens. As he did, the power of God fell, and they dropped to the ground. The teens on the floor began to groan and cry out. Some tried to leave the room before the boy turned and pointed in their direction; but they were unable to move, as if their feet were glued. All of the teens received a wonderful deliverance and experience of God's presence.

As the power of God lifted, I returned to the house. Suddenly, as we were talking about the things that had happened in the chapel, the power of God came into the room and fell upon the adults and they also dropped to the floor. Some laughed, some cried, some were healed and set free.

As the Holy Spirit lifted we heard a commotion from upstairs and many of the children came running down. Some were crying and weeping, others laughing. The Holy Spirit had not left them out just because they were asleep. He had awakened them and touched them also with His mercy and grace.

Man may neglect and consider children of little spiritual value, but, "...there is no partiality with God." (See Romans 2:11.) They are of great important to Him.

—DAVID WALTERS

* * * * * * * * * * * * * * * * *

20/4/1788. (BOLTON) About three I met between **nine hundred and a *thousand of the children*** belonging to our Sunday-schools. I never saw such a sight before. They were all exactly clean, as well as plain in their apparel. All were serious and well-behaved; many, both boys and girls, had beautiful faces as I believe, England or Europe can afford.

When they all sung together, and none of them out of tune, the melody was beyond any theater. And what is best of all, many of them truly fear God, and some rejoice in His salvation. These are a pattern to all the town.

Their usual diversion is, to visit the poor that are sick, (sometimes six or eight, or ten together,) to exhort, comfort and pray with them. Frequently ten or more get together, to sing and pray by themselves: sometimes thirty or forty: and are so earnestly engaged, alternately singing, praying, and crying, that they know not how to part.

You, *children,* that hear this, why would not you go and do likewise? Is not God here, as well as at Bolton? Let God arise, and maintain His own cause! Even "Out of the mouths of babes and sucklings."

10/6/1788. DARLINGTON. Wesley talks with Margaret Barlow, a **girl** of about **fifteen,** who frequently talked with an angel who told her things about to happen.

The accounts you have just read of Wesley's ministry with children is not exhausted. We took only a number for this publication. There are also many other accounts of revival with children and youth, some involving historic preachers and some not; we cannot relate them all, as they are too numerous. The following are worth noting:

DECEMBER 1829. SCOTLAND. In the small Island of Pabay, Loch Roag, there lived a little **girl** whose name was Catherine Smith. Kitty, as she was commonly called, showed herself to be endowed with a truly devotional spirit from her earliest infancy.

The religious atmosphere of her islet home was beautifully reflected in her child-life and spiritual experiences. When only **two years old** she clasped her hands with reverence at family worship. At **three years** she could repeat the 23rd Psalm with such understanding and spiritual relish as proved her to be indeed one of the Good Shepherd's little lambs, and repeated the Lord's prayer regularly, and sometimes in the darkness and silence of the night.

She cultivated the habit of prayer, for which her brothers and sisters often mocked her. She was so filled with love to Christ, and so enthralled by His attractiveness, that she continually spoke of Him to her little companion.

One day she went home greatly downcast saying, "The children vexed me very much today. I will not go with them, for they said that Christ was black, and that grieved my spirit. I told them that Christ was white and glorious in His apparel." (We do not believe this was speaking of His skin color.) Her grief that anyone should speak a disparaging word about Jesus was sufficient proof of her genuine affection for Him.

Her mother, on one occasion, saw her intently gazing into a roaring fire, and asked what she was looking at?

"I am seeing that my state would be awful if I were to fall into that fire, even though I should be immediately taken out," she replied, "But woe is me, those who are cast into hell fire will never come out thence."

On another occasion, she looked over the edge of a precipice, she exclaimed to her mother,

"How fearful would our fate be if we were to fall down this rock, even though we should be lifted up again, but they who are cast into the depths of hell will never be raised there from."

Her parents had heard Dr. MacDonald Ferintosh, preaching at Uig, when he pointed out the danger of formality and want of spirituality in prayer; and that many were content with old, useless, lifeless forms.

As they spoke of it after going home, Kitty said, "It is time for me to give up my old form of prayer."

"Neither you or your prayers are old," chaffed her mother.

But she replied, "I must give them up, and use the prayers which the Lord will teach me."

When she looked gloomy and sad her mother tried to cheer her by jocular remarks, but she answered, "Oh mother you are vexing my spirit; I would rather hear you praying."

Her favorite song was Peter Grant's hymn on "The Blood of Christ." When she came to the concluding verse, which says, "It is not valued according to its worth," she would in touching terms, lament that His blood was so lightly esteemed.

Between the age of seven and eight she was attacked by some disease which was the means of removing her into the Kingdom of Heaven. She pitied most of those she was leaving behind her.

"I pity everyone who is in a Christless state," was her reply.

Towards the end she used to pray, "Oh, Holy One of Israel, save me from death. Oh redeem me from death."

In her last moments, her father leaning over her, said, "Kitty where are you now?"

She replied, "I am on the shore," and immediately her soul was launched into the great ocean of eternity.

GEORGE WHITFIELD IN EDINBURGH SCOTLAND.

George Whitfield preached to the boys of Heriot's Hospital. It was called a hospital because both teachers and pupils ate, slept and lived there, the boys receiving both their education and their maintenance free.

In November one of the masters told a friend about *'the remarkable behavior of his boys,'* some 'who were ringleaders to the rest in vices are now spending their time reading the Bible, and books of piety, and exhorting their fellows to do the like.'

At bedtime, which was 8.00 pm, they were supposed to pray, but while one said the Lord's Prayer the others used to laugh or have a carryon. 'But now, in a calm evening, through every corner of that large house, you may hear little societies worshipping the God and Father of our Lord Jesus Christ, breathing from their souls a warm and holy devotion, till late at night.'

WHITFIELD RETURNED TO EDINBURGH IN 1742 and reported, *"The three little boys* that were converted when I was last here came to me and wept and prayed with me before our Saviour. A minister tells me scarce one is fallen back that were awakened, both amongst old and young."

There are hundreds of accounts of revivals in schools.

WHEN REV. MURRAY MCCHEYNE RETURNED TO DUNDEE IN NOVEMBER 1839, he discovered thirty-nine weekly meetings for prayer in his church, five of them were conducted and attended entirely by *little children.*

IN 1861 God began to move in the **WEST HIGHLANDS OF SCOTLAND** among the *children* who were looking after the sheep on the hills. They read the Bible during the day and met for prayer in barns in the evening. Many *children of ten to twelve years of age* walked seven miles to church twice a week groups which read and sang as they walked.

AROUND THE SAME TIME IN PORTESSIE IN THE DUMFRIES AREA, a work was opened for *180 child* enquirers.

A few years later *8,000 children* gathered to listen to *Edward Payson Hammond at Charles Spurgeon's* church, The Metropolitan Tabernacle, in London.

* * * * * * * * * * * * * * * *

When there is real revival it is always accompanied by a burden for the lost. Back in the early seventies in England many of our church children went witnessing outside the pubs and bars in the local town. Those endeavors resulted in many drug pushers and bar-hoppers finding the Lord. A number of those saved through the children's ministry are now elders in churches today.

DAVID WALTERS

* * * * * * * * * * * * * * * *

FROM 1874-1883 Children's prayer meetings sprang up following D. L. Moody's campaigns in Paisley, Greenock, and Mintlaw.

IN 1939 ON THE ISLAND OF LEWIS there were cottage meetings for **teenagers.** An eyewitness said, "There was such power in the singing that the people went out through the power of the spirit.

Charles Haddon Spurgeon endorsed the ministry of children.

IN APRIL 1868 he advocated lively meetings for the young, with speakers, revival hymns, and 'The liberty of clapping hands and cheering every now and then.'

He advocated prayer meetings for boys and girls and said, 'Never fear precocity, there is much more danger of indifference.' He believed **children** capable of doing their own outreach and of looking after each other pastorally. He concluded, 'We have never devoloped the capabilities of youth as we should have done.'

CONCLUSION

We believe that the God of Wesley, Whitfield, Spurgeon, Hammond, and many others is still moving and desiring to move on our children and youth today.

Wesley says in one account,

"I met a large number of **children** just as much acquainted with God, and the things of God, as 'a wild ass's colt" and just as much concerned about them: and yet who can believe that these pretty little creatures have the 'wrath of God' abiding on them?"

It is hard for our generation to think of little ones on their way to hell. Unfortunately, **children** don't go to heaven because they are pretty and cute. Perhaps that is why we often revert to entertaining, rather than evangelizing our children, or at best, sugar coating the gospel to make it palatable to their desires. Let us now learn from the heroes of the past.

David Walters.

OTHER BOOKS BY DAVID WALTERS

Equipping The Younger Saints.
A guide for teaching children about true salvation and spiritual gifts.

Kids In Combat.
Can our children and youth be used by God to do mighty things? It's time to stop entertaining and start training! Children and teens need to be changed and charged by the power of the Holy Spirit.

The Anointing And You/ Understanding Revival.
David's classic. Claimed to be one of the best books ever written on understanding revival.

So You Think You're a Worshiper?
What is worship? How important is music? David Walters says he may be called a dummy about music, but he knows about the Holy Spirit.

Radical Living in a Godless Society.
Our Godless society really targets our children and youth. How do we cope with this situation?

Living in Revival - *The Everyday Lifestyle Of The Normal Christian.*
Amazing accounts which David and Kathie experienced in the 70's in England. Including Angelic visitations, freedom of the spirit, Divine encounters, Deliverance, Healing, Prosperity and Salvation.

51

Living in the Holy Spirit -*You have the Holy Spirit !*
Does the Holy Spirit Have You?
A revelatory step by step follow-up to The Anointing & You

How to be Ordinary, Average Mediocre & Unsucessful.
An amusing reverse psychology booklet. If you do the opposite to what this booklet proposes, you may be cursed with success.

CHILDREN'S SELF STUDY BIBLE WORKBOOKS (ILLUSTRATED) FOR AGES 6–15

The Armor of God
A children's Bible study based on Ephesians 6:10–18.

Fact or Fantasy?
A study on Christian apologetics (How to defend your faith) designed for children and youth/adults

Being a Christian
A Bible study teaching children and teens how to be a Christian.

Fruit of the Spirit
A study teaching children and teens how to be a fruitful Christian.

Children's Prayer Manual
Children's illustrated study on prayer (ages 7–14 years).

The Gifts of the Spirit
Children's illustrated Bible study on the gifts of the Spirit (ages 7 years–adult).

Children's Fantasy Adventure Books

The Book of Funtastic Adventures

Bedtime stories to make children & parents laugh
Eleven imaginary stories of David's two grandsons as
Jedi knights having amazing hilarious adventures with
Superheroes & story book characters. Ages 8-14

The 2nd Book of Funtastic Adventures

More hilarious adventures of David's two grandsons as
Jedi Knights traveling through space with Moses their
robot pilot searching for their parents and sister who
have been kidnapped by aliens. Ages 8-14

The Funtastic Adventure of Inisfree
David's grand daughter has her own funy and exciting
adventures as one of her brothers is kidnapped by aliens
to be sold as a slave on planet, "Bizzare" and she has to
rescue him.

The Adventures of Tiny the Bear

An amusing set of stories how a bear helps children
deal with name calling and bullying. Ages 6-11

BOOKS BY KATHIE WALTERS

ANGELS WATCHING OVER YOU
Did you know that angels are very active in our everyday lives?

THE BRIGHT AND SHINING REVIVAL
An account of the Hebrides Revival 1948–1952.

CELTIC FLAMES
Read the exciting accounts of famous fourth- and fifth-century Celtic Christians: Patrick, Brendan, and others.

COLUMBA—THE CELTIC DOVE
Read about the ministry of this famous Celtic Christian, filled with supernatural visitations.

PARENTING BY THE SPIRIT
The author shows how she raised her children by listening to the Holy Spirit rather than her emotions.

LIVING BY THE SUPERNATURAL
How to live in our inheritance—supernaturally.

THE SPIRIT OF FALSE JUDGMENT
In the light of holy revelation, sometimes things are different from what we perceive them to be.

THE VISITATION
Supernatural visitations of a mother and daughter.

PROGEST...WHAT?
Read about the great benefits of natural progesterone.

ELITISM AND THE SPIRIT OF CONTROL
How the spirit of control comes into a church.

WHAT HAPPENED TO EVAN ROBERTS?
Evan Roberts the vessle that God used in the mighty 1904 Welsh revival. What caused the revival to leave and Evan Roberts have five nervous breakdowns.

THE SPIRITUAL MEANING OF AROMA, COLORS, FLOWERS & TREES
Have you ever wondered what different aromas,and visions of flowers, trees a nd colors mean.

CD's & DVD's by David Walters

Children Aflame

Born in the War Zone

Breaking Traditional Barriers in Children's Ministry

Fact or Fiction?

The Solution

Called or Chosen?

Raising Godly Children and Teens

The Anointed Generation

Bringing Forth Children of Destiny

Foolish Things

Battle for the Seed

Equipping the Younger Saints 3CD set

The Book of Funtastic Adventures Audio Set 4 CD's 11 stories

DVD's

**Raising a Generation of Anointed Families
4DVD set**

Power Principles for Parents &Teachers

Children in Intercession

How to Reach Lost Church Kids

**Raising a Generation of Anointed
Children and Youth 4 Parts 2 DVD's**

David Walters Teaching & Miracle Meeting DVD

**Check out David's website for e-books
davidwaltersministry.com**

Teaching CD's
By Kathie Walters

In Depth for Seers & Prophets 3 CD set

Getting Free from Religious Spirits

David's Mighty Men

The Almond Tree

Revival Accounts

Faith & Angels 2 CD Set

The Glory Realm 2 CD Set

Spiritual Abortion 2 CD Set

Satans Strategies 3 CD Set

Fanatic in the Attic

DVD

Living in the Glory Conference 5 DVD Set

**Check out Kathie's website for e-books
kathiewaltersministry.com**

GOOD NEWS FELLOWSHIP MINISTRIES
220 Sleepy Creek Road, Macon, GA 31210
Telephone: (478) 757-8071

E-mail: www.goodnews@usa.com
www.davidwaltersministry.com

ABOUT THE WALTERS
FAMILY

David and Kathie Walters are originally from England. They have lived and ministered in the United States for over thirty years. They presently reside in Macon, Georgia.

They oversee Good News Ministries. They have two daughters, two grandsons, and a granddaughter.

David has a burden for what he terms as "church-wise" kids and teens—those who have been brought up in the church and who have a head knowledge only of the things of God. His desire is for the young people to have a dynamic experience of God for themselves.

His "Raising Anointed Children and Youth & Holy Spirit Family Encounters" are for church leaders, youth pastors, parents, children and teens. He also holds revival meetings for churches and includes the children and teens in the miracle ministry of the Holy Spirit. David has ministered at many national conferences in the U.S. and overseas.

Kathie ministers at churches, fellowships conferences and retreats. She has a desire to see Christians forth in all of their anointings and giftings. She believes that the realm of the Spirit, the supernatural power of God, heaven and angels are our inheritance and are meant to be a normal part of our lives and the life of the church.

She also believes in Spirit-led parenting. She has been interviewed several times on "It's Supernatural" TV program with Sid Roth. She has also traveled to many countries bringing revvial to many people and churches.

BOOKING
INFORMATION

GOOD NEWS FELLOWSHIP
MINISTRIES
220 Sleepy Creek Road, Macon, GA
31210
Telephone: (478)757-8071

E-mail:
davidmwalters@mindspring.com

David and Kathie Walters both minister out of
Good News Ministries in the United States and
overseas.
For further information write or call
GOOD NEWS MINISTRIES
220 Sleepy Creek Road • Macon, GA 31210
Web-site: www.kathiewaltersministry.com
Good News Ministries e-mail:
goodnewsministeries@usa.com
David's e-mail:
davidmwalters@mindspring.com
Kathie's e-mail:
kathiewalters@mindspring.com

Holy Spirit Revival Encounters"
for the Whole Family
Pastors, Youth Pastors, Children's Pastors
Sunday School Teachers, Children's Workers, Nursery
Workers, Children, Teens, Single Adults, Parents,
Grandparents & Grandchildren.

The churches in your area can experience one of these dynamic Events. Author, speaker and revivalist, David Walters, imparts a fresh vision and anointing to everyone including those who work with children and youth. Walters says:

"Children do not have a baby or junior Holy Spirit!"
"Children are baptized in the Holy Spirit to do much more than play, be entertained or listen to a few moral object lessons!"

"The average church-wise child can be turned around and set on fire for God!"
"Christian teenagers do not have to surrender to peer pressure—they can become the peers!"
Families can be transformed.

TOURS OF IRELAND AND SCOTLAND
with Kathie Walters

Come to Ireland and Scotland on a 10-Day Celtic Heritage Tour with Kathie Walters!

• Re-dig the spiritual wells of this beautiful country.

• Pray on the Hill of Slane where St. Patrick lit his Pascal fire and defied the High King.

• See the place where St. Patrick first landed to bring the Gospel to Ireland by God through the angel of Ireland, Victor.

• See the green hills and dales of Ireland—a picture you will never forget.

• Visit the ancient places of worship that will help enable you to grasp hold of your godly inheritance.

Then on to Scotland

• Tour the beautiful highlands of Scotland.

• Visit the island of Iona, where St. Columba built his monastery.

• Tour the Hebrides Islands. (Visit the church and talk to the people who were in the great revival there during 1949–1952.)